Leigh-Preston – UK

Photography Yearbook 1994

Internationales Jahrbuch der Fotografie 1994

PHOTOG

YEAR

INTERNATIONALES
JAHRBUCH
DER FOTOGRAFIE

GRAPHY BOOK 1994

Edited by Peter Wilkinson FRPS

 FOUNTAIN PRESS

FOUNTAIN PRESS LIMITED
Queensborough House
2 Claremont Road
Surbiton
Surrey
England
KT6 4QU

© FOUNTAIN PRESS 1993
ISBN 0 86343 311 1

Designed by Grant Bradford

Typesetting by Rex Carr

Reproduction and Printing by
Regent Publishing Services Ltd
Hong Kong & Singapore

Deutsche Ausgabe:
©1993 Wilhelm Knapp Verlag,
Niederlassung der Droste Verlag GmbH, Düsseldorf.
ISBN 3 87420 174 0

CONTENTS

Introduction

6

The Photographers

12

The Photographs

17

Technical Data

226

INTRODUCTION

When considering the many thousands of pictures submitted for the Photography Yearbook I rarely have any idea as to the nationality or the name of the author and so it is a constant surprise to discover that a photograph of an English garden has been taken by a Japanese, that pictures of New York are by a German and a picture of a Venetian festival by a Norwegian. This leads me to assume that there are a large number of photographers who do not consider familiar faces and places to be photogenic and that most of their serious photography takes place when they are on vacation or working in an unfamiliar environment. I find this understandable as to some extent my own photography has suffered from this narrow outlook.

The unique appeal of the images submitted by photographers from eastern European countries in the past has been their spontaneity often combined with a subtle touch of humour and sympathetic recording of their environment. These attributes are frequently lacking in pictures from photographers from other countries and it occurs to me that, because of travel restrictions, eastern European photographers have had to find their subjects in their own 'back-yards' with surprisingly interesting results.

Because an area or subject is familiar it is easy to be blind to its photographic potential, although to others, less acquainted, it would be of pictorial and general interest. So now is the time for photographers in countries effected by recession, with consequential shortage of money to spend on travel, not to curtail their photography, but to emulate their eastern European colleagues by looking nearer to home for their subjects.

Hopefully, we look forward to seeing some of the results in future editions of the Photography Yearbook.

The publisher and I are delighted that we have had such a superb submission of pictures from photographers from many countries for this edition of the book and we thank them all for their support. Congratulations to those who have been successful; with such a large entry it is inevitable that many excellent pictures could not be included and we trust that those who were unsuccessful will not be too disappointed and will support us again in the future.

Peter Wilkinson FRPS
EDITOR

Fountain Press are always pleased to receive pictures for possible inclusion in future editions of Photography Yearbook and to retain the international character of the book entries from outside the U.K. countries are especially welcome.

Although material can be sent at any time throughout the year the closing date for receiving material at the publishers for possible inclusion in the next edition of Photography Yearbook is the end of January 1994 and this will apply in subsequent years.

Colour transparencies may be of any size but should not be glass mounted. If a colour picture is available both as a print and as a transparency, the transparency is preferred. Prints, both black and white and colour, should be unmounted and not smaller than 18 x 24cm or larger than 30 x 40cm. Prints should always be packed flat not rolled. All work submitted must carry the author's name, and information is required as to the location or subject and any points of interest relating to the picture as well as to the make of camera, lens and film used.

If packing is suitable, and adequate return postage in Sterling cheques (plus 60p Bank handling charge), Sterling stamps or money orders or twelve International Reply Coupons is included, work will be returned after the book has been finalised. Non United Kingdom entries will be returned by surface mail unless sufficient additional remittance is included to cover air mail.

All possible care will be taken by Fountain Press but they cannot be held responsible for any loss or damage that might occur to material submitted. Although the copyright of any work accepted remains with the author, the publisher reserves the right to use accepted pictures to publicise Photography Yearbook.

As well as the prestige of having their work published, successful contributors will also receive a copy of Photography Yearbook and a reproduction fee. Upon request the Publisher will, where possible, put prospective picture buyers in touch with the authors of successful pictures.

EINLEITUNG

Das vorliegende Fotografische Jahrbuch ist eine Auswahl und zugleich Spiegelbild dessen, was mir diesmal an vielfältigem Fotomaterial zur Verfügung gestellt wurde. Aufgrund der Beiträge unterscheidlichster Fotografen und Nationalitäten ist es nicht verwunderlich, ein Foto eines englischen Gartens zu entdecken, das von einem Japaner aufgenommen wurde. Ebenfalls sind Bilder aus New York von einem Deutschen, oder ein Foto eines Norwegers von einem Festival in Venedig vorzufinden.

Dies läßt vermuten, daß viele Fotografen nicht nur ihr familiäres Umfeld als fotogen betrachten, sondern hauptsächlich während des Urlaubs oder auch während der Arbeit fotografieren. Dafür habe ich großes Verständnis, da meine Fotos in gewissem Maße ebenfalls von diesem beschränkten Blickwinkel geprägt sind.

Die Eindrücke, die in der Vergangenheit von den Fotografen aus osteuropäischen Ländern vermittelt wurden, zeugen von einer genialen Kombination aus Spontanität, einer feinen Spur Humor und einer verständnisvollen Aufnahme ihrer Umwelt. Diese Akzente fehlen häufig bei Fotografen aus anderen Ländern.

Aufgrund der Reisebeschränkung osteuropäischer Fotografen konzentrieren sich viele auf Motive in ihrem Umfeld und erzielen dabei überraschend interessante Ergebnisse.

Bei einer vertrauten Umgebung ist es häufig schwierig, das fotografische Potential zu erkennen. Bei weniger Bekanntem hingegen ist das Interesse, etwas im Bild festzuhalten, wesentlich größer. Für Fotografen der Länder, die von der derzeitigen Rezension betroffen sind, und demzufolge auch Konsequenzen für deren Reiseverhalten mit sich bringt, ist die Zeit gekommen, in der sie nicht ihr Fotografiekontingent kürzen, sondern viel mehr ihren osteuropäischen Kollegen nacheifern sollten, indem sie sich die Motive in ihrer Umgebung suchen.

Erwartungsvoll schauen wir in die Zukunft und hoffen einige Ergebnisse in den nächsten Ausgaben des Fotografischen Jahrbuchs zu finden.

Der Verleger und ich sind erfreut, daß wir eine solch großartige Vielfalt an Fotos von Fotografen aus vielen Ländern für diese Ausgabe gewinnen konnten. Wir danken Ihnen alle für ihre Unterstützung.

Gratulationen all denen, die erfolgreich waren. Bei dieser Vielzahl von Einsendungen war es allerdings unvermeidlich, einige exzellente Fotos unberücksichtigt zu lassen. Wir hoffen, daß die Betroffenen nicht allzu sehr enttäuscht sind, und rechnen auch in Zukunft mit Ihrer Unterstützung.

Peter Wilkinson FRPS
HERAUSGEBER

Einsendeschluß für Material, das möglicherweise in der nächsten Ausgabe des Internationalen Jahrbuchs der Fotografie veröffentlicht wird, ist Ende Januar 1994. Zu diesem Zeitpunkt muß das Material beim Verleger eingelangt sein. Farbtransparente können von jeglicher Größe sein, dürfen jedoch nicht in Glasrahmen gesandt werden. Sollte ein Farbbild als Abzug und als Farbtransparent vorhanden sein, bitten wir um Einsendung des Dias. Alle Fotos - sowohl Schwarz/Weiß als auch Farb - sollen nicht aufgezogen, nicht kleiner als 18 x 24cm und nicht größer als 30 x 40cm sein. Abzüge sollen immer flach verpackt und nicht gerollt werden. Alle eingesandten Arbeiten müssen den Namen des Fotografen tragen, sowie Informationen über Aufnahmeort, spezielle Interessensfaktoren in Bezug auf die Aufnahme und vor allem Angaben über die verwendete Kamera, Linse und Film enthalten.

Wenn das Verspackungsmaterial entspricht und ausreichendes Retourporto in Form von Schecks in Englischen Pfunden oder Internationalen Antwortscheinen beigelegt ist, werden Arbeiten nach Verlagsabschluß des Buches retourniert. Fountain Press wird selbstverständlich alle arbeiten mit größter Sorgfalt behandeln, kann jedoch keinerlei Haftung für eventuelle Beschädigung oder Verluste des eingesandten Materials übernehmen. Wenn auch das Urheberrect der eingesandten Arbeiten dem Einsender zusteht, darf der Verleger angenommene Arbeiten im Internationalen Jahrbuch der Fotografie veröffentlichen.

Abgesehen vom Prestige ihre Arbeiten veröffentlicht zu sehen, werden erfolgreiche Teilnehmer auch eine Ausgabe des Internationalen Jahrbuchs der Fotografie und eine Reproduktionsgebühr erhalten. Auf Anfrage wird sich der Verlag bemühen, zukünftige Fotokäufer und Schöpfer erfolgreicher Bilder zusammenzuführen.

Wir hoffen, daß Sie am Internationalen Jahrbuch der Fotografie 1994 Freude haben und auch in Zukunft Ihre Arbeiten für mögliche Publikation in der nächsten Ausgabe einsenden werden. Fotos von Fotografen außerhalb Großbritanniens sind uns besonders willkommen, da diese helfen, den Internationalen Charakter dieses Buches aufrechtzuerhalten.

INTRODUCTION

En examinant les milliers d'images proposées pour le Photography Yearbook, il est rare que je puisse avoir la moindre idée du nom ou de la nationalité de leurs auteurs, et ce m'est toujours une surprise de découvrir qu'une photographie d'un jardin anglais est l'oeuvre d'un Japonais, des images de New York, l'oeuvre d'un Allemand, des vues d'un festival vénitien, celle d'un Norvégien. Ceci me conduit à supposer que nombre de photographes ne considèrent pas les visages ou les lieux familiers comme photogéniques, et que c'est en vacances, ou lorsqu'ils travaillent dans un environnement étranger, qu'ils pratiquent leur photographie le plus sérieusement. Ce que d'ailleurs je comprends fort bien, car dans une certaine mesure, ma propre photographie a souffert de cette même étroitesse de vue.

L'unique attrait des images soumises jusqu'à présent par les photographes des pays d'Europe de l'Est a été leur spontanéité, colorée souvent d'un subtil humour, et reflétant avec sympathie le milieu familier. Ces qualités sont souvent absentes des travaux proposés par les photographes des autres pays, et je me demande si les photographes de l'Europe de l'Est ne se sont pas trouvés, à cause des restrictions imposées aux voyages, dans la nécessité de chercher leurs sujets dans leur propre 'arrière-cour', et ceci avec des résultats remarquablement intéressants.

Il est facile de rester aveugle au potentiel photographique d'un lieu ou d'un sujet familiers, lesquels peuvent offrir à ceux qui les connaissent moins, un intérêt pictorial ou général. Aussi le temps est-il peut-être venu, pour les photographes des pays affectés par la recession, et les difficultés financières frappant les possibilités de voyages, non pas de restreindre leur activité photographique, mais d'imiter leurs collègues d'Europe de l'Est, et de chercher le sujet de leurs travaux tout près de chez eux. Nous espérons voir dans les prochaines éditions du Photography Yearbook les résultats de cette recherche.

Les éditeurs de Fountain Press et moi-même sommes très heureux du superbe envoi d'images proposées pour cette édition, par de si nombreux photographes de si nombreux pays, et nous les remercions tous de leur appui. Nous félicitons ceux dont les travaux ont été choisis; avec de si nombreux envois, il est inévitable que beaucoup d'excellentes photographies n'aient pu être incluses, et nous esperons que ceux dont les travaux n'ont pas été choisis ne seront pas trop déçus et continueront à nous donner leur appui.

Peter Wilkinson FRPS
EDITEUR

La date limite pour la réception des travaux soumis en veu d'une eventuelle publication dans le Photography Yearbook est le 31 janvier 1994, et ceci s'applique, mutatis mutandis, aux années suivantes. Les diapositives en couleurs peuvent être de n'importent quelles dimensions, mais ne doivent pas être montées sur verre. Au cas où une photographie en couleurs existe à la fois en épreuve et en diapositive, la diapositive sera préférée. Les épreuves, en blanc et noir ou en couleurs, ne doivent pas être montées, et ne doivent pas mesurer moins de 18 x 24cm, ni plus de 30 x 40cm. Les épreuves doivent toujours être emballées à plat, non roulées. Tous les travaux proposés doivent porter le nom de leur auteur, et l'indication du lieu, et d'autres faits relatifs à l'image, a l'appareil à l'objectif et à la pellicule utilisés.

Si l'emballage est convenable, et l'envoi accompagné des frais de port sous forme de chèque ou de mandat sterling, ou de douze Coupons Réponse Internationaux, les travaux seront réexpédiés à leurs auteurs une fois achevée la préparation du livre. Les travaux reçus de pays autres que le Royaume-Uni seront renvoyés par courrier ordinaire à moins qu'ils ne soient accompagnés d'une somme suffisante à couvrir les frais de courrier par avion.

Bien que tous les envois soient traités avec le plus grand soin, Fountain Press ne peut accepter la responsabilité d'aucune perte ou dommage survenus au matériel reçu. Et bien que le copyright de toutes les photographies soit conservé par l'auteur, les éditeurs se réservent le droit de les utiliser à des fins de publicité pour le Photography Yearbook. Les contributeurs dont les travaux sont reproduits non seulement jouiront du prestige que leur confère la publication dans le Photography Yearbook, mais aussi recevront un exemplaire du livre et un droit de reproduction. Sur requête, la direction de Fountain Press pourra se charger, là où il sera possible, de mettre en relation les éventuels acheteurs avec les auteurs des photographies publiées.

INTRODUCCION

A la hora de considerar las miles de fotografías presentadas al Photography Yearbook, desconozco por lo general la nacionalidad y el nombre del autor/a. Por tanto, es con gran sorpresa que descubro a veces que la fotografía de un jardín inglés ha sido tomada por un japonés, las fotografías de Nueva York por un alemán y las de un festival en Venecia por un noruego. Esto me lleva a pensar que, para muchos de nuestros fotógrafos, las caras y los lugares más conocidos son los menos fotogénicos y que su trabajo más importante se realiza cuando están de vacaciones o trabajando en ambientes desconocidos. Pero este hecho no me sorprende totalmente ya que mis propias fotografías sufren a veces de este enfoque restringido

La mayor atracción de las imágenes presentadas por fotógrafos de Europa del este en el pasado ha sido su espontaneidad combinada con un ligero toque de humor y un reflejo comprensivo y sincero del ambiente que les rodea. Estas cualidades faltan a veces en las obras presentadas por fotógrafos de otros países y se me ocurre que, debido a la falta de libertad para viajar, los fotógrafos de Europa del este han tenido que buscar sus sujetos a la puerta de sus casas con resultados a menudo sorprendentes.

Cuando un lugar o sujeto nos son conocidos, es muy fácil no ver el potencial fotográfico que para otros, desde fuera, pueden tener como objetos de interés general y artístico. Ha llegado pues el momento de que, en los países afectados por la recesión económica, con menores recursos para viajar, los fotógrafos sigan trabajando y, al igual que sus colegas en Europa del este, busquen sus sujetos cerca de sus puertas.

Esperamos pues ver los resultados en las próximas ediciones del Photography Yearbook.

El editor y yo nos sentimos muy felices con el gran número de excelentes fotografías presentadas a la presente edición por fotógrafos de muchos países y deseamos agradecerles su colaboración. Felicidades a los ganadores; con una selección tan variada es inevitable que no se puedan incluir muchas de las obras que bien lo merecieran, y esperamos que los participantes que no han ganado en esta ocasión no se sientan demasiado desilusionados y nos sigan apoyando en el futuro.

Peter Wilkinson FRPS
REDACTOR GENERAL

El plazo para recibir material para su posible inclusión en la próxima edición del Photography Yearbook se cierra el 31 de enero de 1994, y esto se aplicará a los años subsiguientes.

Las transparencias en color pueden ser de cualquier tamaño pero no montadas en vidrio. Si las fotogrofías en color existen como copia en papel y como transparencia, preferimos la transparencia. Las copias en papel, ya sean en blanco y negro o en color, deberán ir sin borde y tener un mínimo de 18 x 24cm y un máximo de 30 x 40cm. Las copias en papel deberán ir siempre enviadas de forma plana, no enrolladas. Todas las obras presentadas llevarán el nombre del autor y cualquier tipo de información relativa al lugar o sujeto fotografiados, así como cualquier punto de interés relativo a la fotografía, el tipo y marca de cámara, lente y película empleada

Si el embalaje es adecuado para su devolución y se cubren los gastos de envío con un cheque en libras esterlinas, giro postal o doce Cupones de Envío Internacional, las obras serán devueltas una vez hecha la selección y terminado el libro. Las participaciones de fuera del Reino Unido serán devueltas por correo ordinario o no ser que se cubran los gastos adicionales de correo aéreo.

Aunque se tomarán las medidas adecuadas, Fountain Press no se hace responsable de ninguna pérdida o daño que pueda sufrir el material. Aunque los derechos de autor sobre las obras seleccionadas seguirán en posesión del mismo, el editor se reserva el derecho a utilizarlas como publicidad del Photography Yearbook.

Los fotógrafos que sean seleccionados recibirán, además del prestigio de ser incluidos en sus páginas, una copia del Photography Yearbook y honorarios por cada reproducción. De ser requerido, y siempre que sea posible, la editorial pondrá en contacto a futuros compradores con los autores de las fotografías seleccionadas.

BRIAN BOWER FRPS

THE ROYAL PHOTOGRAPHIC SOCIETY

GET ON THE ROAD TO SUCCESS!

For 139 years THE ROYAL PHOTOGRAPHIC SOCIETY has been helping photographers of all ages and all abilities to successfully develop the potential of their photography. Whether you are a total beginner, a dedicated amateur or someone who earns a living from full-time work in the photographic world, membership of the Society is an open road to achievement.

As a member of the Society you are entitled to submit work for the Licentiateship, Associateship and in due course, Fellowship, the three distinctions that the Society offers. All over the world people who hold distinctions of the Society are recognised as high achievers in the art or science of photography.

The Society actively encourages and supports its members as they work towards distinctions, and membership provides the opportunity to become part of a wide network of fellow photographers. There are workshops, lectures, master classes, conferences, field trips and informal meetings; in fact The Royal Photographic Society has something new happening almost every day. As a member you will receive quarterly the complete national Programme guide to over 600 events that the Society organises each year.

Other benefits that the Society provides are the two magazines, the Photographic Journal which is a lively and informative periodical with debates on controversial aspects of photography and reviews and views on the latest in art and technology and The Journal of Photographic Science which is a more specialised magazine and one which

ERIC HOWARD

discusses the current developments at the frontier of imaging science.

As soon as you apply for membership you will receive your New Members' Pack which will give you full information on membership , information about the Society's permanent Collection, the exhibitions, discounts negotiated for members, and the fourteen special interest Groups.

Membership of The Royal Photographic Society is an adventure to new horizons. There are many positive reasons for joining the Society so let us light your pathway to success! Readers of "PHOTOGRAPHY YEARBOOK" are being given the opportunity of three months' free membership! Join now and receive fifteen months' membership for the price of twelve. Write now to the Membership Officer,
THE ROYAL PHOTOGRAPHIC SOCIETY,
Milsom Street, Bath. BA1 1DN.
(Telephone 0225 462841 or Fax 0225 448688)
Be sure to mark your request (PYB'94)

THE PHOTOGRAPHERS

Ulrich Ackermann - Switzerland	114, 115, 214, 215	
Nigel Amies - UK	220, 221	
John Anthony - UK	132, 133	
Victor Attfield - UK	48	
Robert Bailly - France	166	
Ian Ball - UK	160	
Carolyn Bates - UK	24, 25	
Malcolm Beaumont - UK	18, 19	
Sue Bennett - UK	124, 125	
Lisa Benstead - UK	150, 151	
Augusto de Bernardi - Italy	122, 123	
James Bidgood - UK	186/187	
Dhiman Bose - India	56, 57, 174/175	
Edward Boutilier - Canada	157	
John Bullough - UK	196	
Barbro Bunnage - UK	17	
Rosemary Calvert - UK	82, 83	
Laurie Campbell - UK	218, 219	
Carlo Chinca - UK	74, 75, 197	
Ivan Cisar - Czech Republic	65, 163	
Donald Clements - UK	217	
David Cooke - UK	30	
Anne Crabbe - UK	40	
Roger Cracknell - UK	22	
Damian Debski - UK	148	
Carli Dietmar - Austria	118, 119	
Phil Dolby - UK	20	
Pavlo Drobjak - Ukraine	106, 107	
Rod Edwards - UK	33	
Roy Elwood - UK	38, 39	
John Evans - UK	184	
Paul Evison - UK	161	

Johann Froschauer - Austria	86	
Alex Fyfe - UK	129, 170/171	
Peter Gedeon - Hungary	180	
Ian George - UK	32	
George Ghiz - Canada	117	
Chris Gleave - UK	34, 35	
Clare Glenister - UK	116	
Claudia Goetzelmann - Germany	223	
John Gray - UK	222	
Van Greaves - UK	155	
Athanas Gritzer - Austria	90, 91, 128	
Krzsztof Grzelak - Poland	176	
Harry Hall - UK	224	
Tony Hamblin - UK	188, 189	
Roger Hance - UK	108	
Clive Harrison - UK	36, 37, 172, 173	
Peter Hense - Germany	198, 199	
Manfred Hermann - Germany	112/113	
Chris Hinterobermaier - Austria	110, 111	
Andy Hoets - USA	102/103	
Mike Hollist - UK	144, 145	
Hezy Holzman - Israel	212, 213	
Chris Howes - UK	46, 47, 164	
Arnold Hubbard - UK	200, 201	
Bill Ivy - Canada	152, 153	
E.A. Janes - UK	88	
Bela Jansky - USA	165	
Peter Jeffery - UK	31	
Max Johnson - Australia	104, 105	
Mike Keegan - UK	63, 93	
Viktor Kolpakov - Latvia	44, 45	
Eugeni Komarov - Ukraine	64	

THE PHOTOGRAPHERS

Rostvslav Kondrat - Ukraine   167

Robert Kralka - Canada   126, 127

Robert Kudlik - Switzerland   87

Pavel Kunin - Kazakhstan   136, 137

Eric Lancaster - UK   177

Markus Lauboeck - Austria   140

Umberto Leonini - Italy   192

Kazimieras Linkevicius
- Lithuania   78

Aleksandras Macijauskas
- Lithuania   202, 203

Bretislav Marek - Czech Republic   182, 183

Julie Meech - UK   149

Graham Merry - Canada   158

Alan Millward - UK   206, 207

Hugh Milsom - UK   66, 168, 169

Paul Mount - UK   62

Bob Mossel - Australia   156

Roger Noons - UK   Front Cover, 96, 209

Andreas Orfanos - Canada   52, 53

Leonid Padrul - Ukraine   70/71

Boris Panov - Ukraine   134/135

Giuseppe Pappalardo - Italy   194/195

John Philpott - UK   162

Manfred Pillik - Austria   120

Malcolm Pleasants - UK   81

Fritz Pölking - Germany   89, 178, 179

Fabio Ponzio - Italy   109

Leigh Preston - UK   Front Endpaper, 142/143

Paul Proctor - UK   190, 191

Norman Prue - UK   29, 60/61, 185

Romualdas Rakauskas - Lithuania   97

Den Reader - UK   54, 55

Kenneth Reay - UK   50, 51

Roger Reynolds - UK   28, 146, 147

Peter Roche - UK   94, 95

Reinhold Rothschedl - Austria   141

Tim Rudman - UK   41, 76, 77

Andrzej Sawa - South Africa   49, 159

Brian Scott - Australia   130, 131, 204, 205

Richard Searle - UK   80

Nigel Shuttleworth - UK   23

Peter Siviter - UK   92

Jill Sneesby - South Africa   26

Ray Spence - UK   67

Jan Svendsen - Norway   121

Cecile Tait - UK   28

Lip Seng Tan - Singapore   216

Mike Taylor - UK   84, 85

Brian Tuff - UK   68, 69, 98, 99

Joe Tymkow - UK   138/139

Sergei Vosiliev - Russia   79

Ferenc Wagner - Hungary   72, 73

Chris Wainwright - UK   110, 111

Gan Feng Wang - Canada   42, 43, 100, 101, 193

Anthony Wharton - UK   21, 154

Barrie Wilkins - South Africa   27, 210, 211

Andy Wilson - UK   208

Steve Woodgate - UK   Back Endpaper

Frank Young - UK   58, 59

THE PHOTOGRAPHS

Barbro Bunnage - UK

17

Malcolm Beaumont - UK

18

Phil Dolby - UK

Anthony Wharton - UK

Roger Cracknell - UK

Nigel Shuttleworth - UK

23

Jill Sneesby - South Africa

26

Barrie Wilkins - South Africa

Roger Reynolds - UK

28

Norman Prue - UK

David Cooke - UK

Peter Jeffery - UK

31

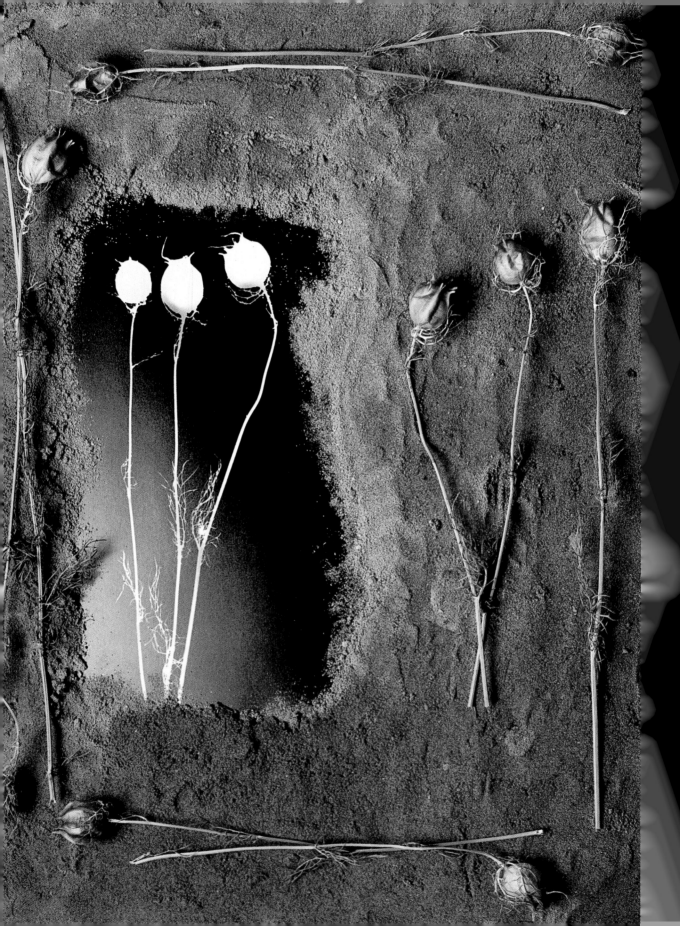

Ian George - UK

Rod Edwards - UK

Chris Gleave - UK

Chris Gleave - UK

Clive Harrison - UK

Clive Harrison - UK

Roy Elwood - UK

Anne Crabbe - UK

Tim Rudman - UK

41

Gang Feng Wang - Canada

Viktor Kolpakov - Latvia

44

Chris Howes - UK

Victor Attfield - UK

Andrzej Sawa - South Africa

49

Kenneth Reay - UK

Kenneth Reay - UK

Andreas Orfanos - Canada

52

Den Reader - UK

54

Den Reader - UK

55

Dhiman Bose - India

Frank Young - UK

58

Frank Young - UK

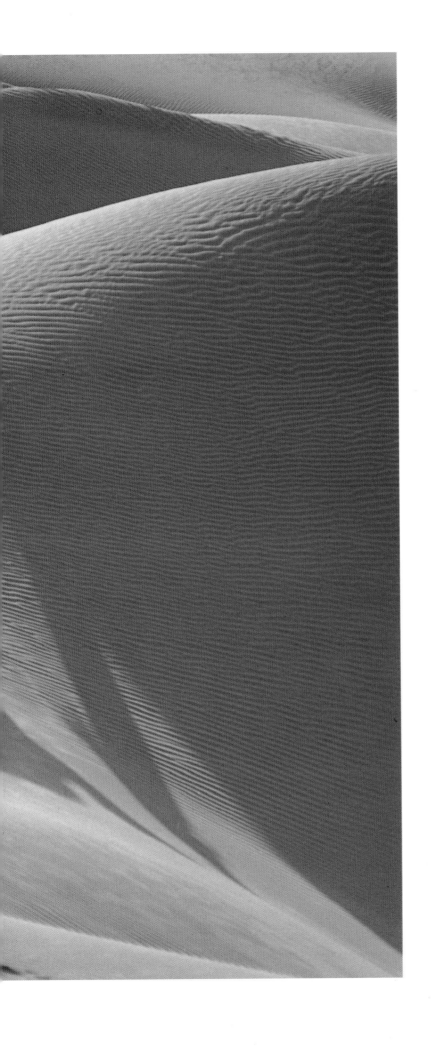

Norman Prue - UK

Paul Mount - UK

Mike Keegan - UK

Eugeni Komarov - Ukraine

Ivan Cisar - Czech Republic

Hugh Milsom - UK

66

Ray Spence - UK

Brian Tuff - UK

68

Brian Tuff - UK

69

Leonid Padrul - Ukraine

Ferenc Wagner - Hungary

Carlo Chinca - UK

74

Carlo Chinca - UK

Tim Rudman - UK

Kazimieras Linkevicius - Lithuania

Sergei Vosiliev - Russia

78

Richard Searle - UK

Malcolm Pleasants - UK

Rosemary Calvert - UK

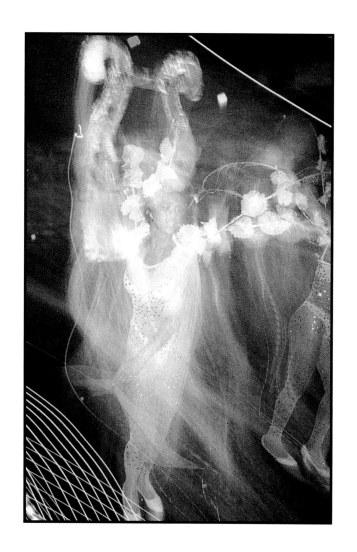

Mike Taylor - UK

84

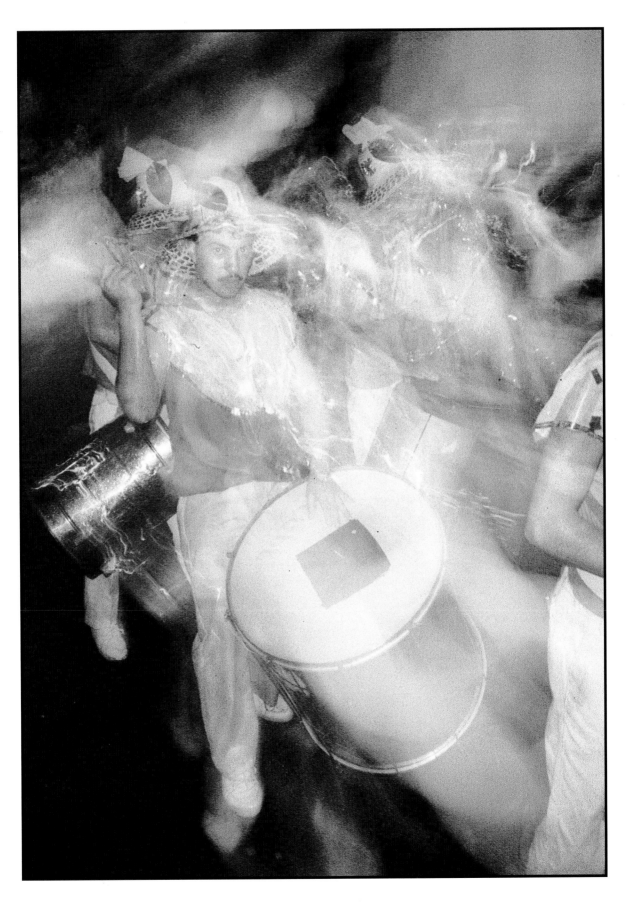

Mike Taylor - UK

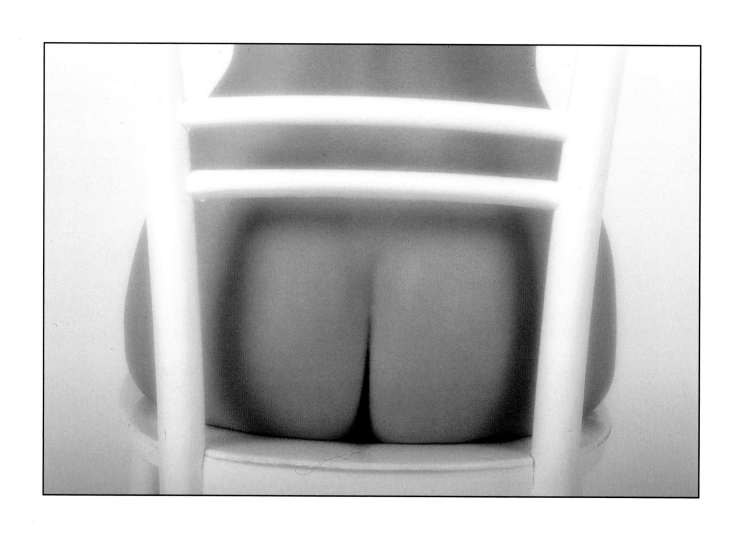

Johann Froschauer - Austria

86

Robert Kudlik - Switzerland

Fritz Pölking - Germany

88

E.A. Janes - UK

89

Athanas Gritzer - Austria

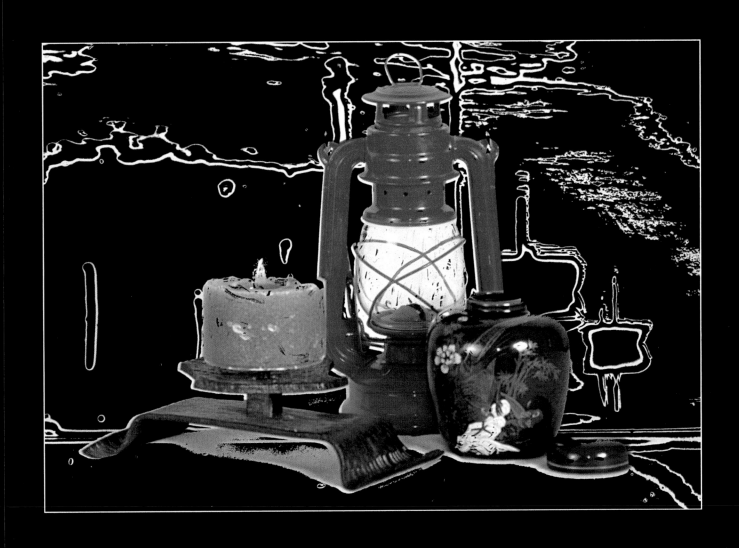

Athanas Gritzer - Austria

Peter Siviter - UK

Mike Keegan - UK

Peter Roche - UK

94

Roger Noons - UK

96

Romualdas Rakauskas - Lithuania

Brian Tuff - UK

99

Gang Feng Wang - Canada

Gang Feng Wang - Canada

Andy Hoets - USA

102

Max Johnson - Australia

104

Max Johnson - Australia

Pavlo Drobjak - Ukraine

Roger Hance - UK

Fabio Ponzio - Italy

109

Chris Hinterobermaier - Austria

Chris Hinterobermaier - Austria

Manfred Hermann - Germany

Ulrich Ackermann - Switzerland

114

Clare Glenister - UK

George Ghiz - Canada

Carli Dietmar - Austria

118

Carli Dietmar - Austria

119

Manfred Pillik - Austria

120

Jan Svendsen - Norway

Augusto de Bernardi - Italy

Augusto de Bernardi - Italy

123

Sue Bennett - UK

124

Sue Bennett - UK

125

Robert Kralka - Canada

Athanas Gritzer - Austria

Alex Fyfe - UK

Brian Scott - Australia

132

John Anthony - UK

Boris Panov - Ukraine

Pavel Kunin - Kazakhstan

6

Joe Tymkow - UK

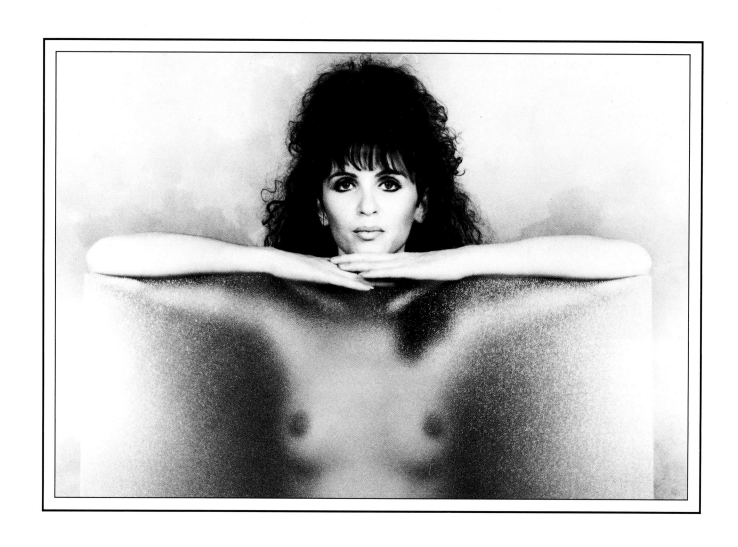

Markus Lauboeck - Austria

Reinhold Rothschedl - Austria

140

Leigh Preston - UK

Mike Hollist - UK

144

Mike Hollist - UK

145

Roger Reynolds - UK

146

Roger Reynolds - UK

147

Damian Debski - UK

Julie Meech - UK

Lisa Benstead - UK

150

Lisa Benstead - UK

151

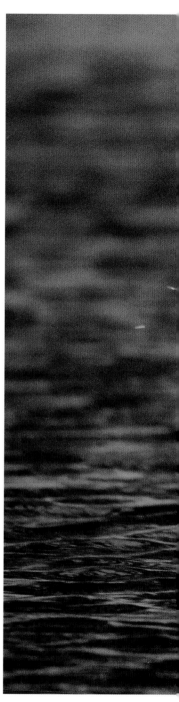

Bill Ivy - Canada

152

Bill Ivy - Canada

153

Anthony Wharton - UK

154

Van Greaves - UK

155

Bob Mossel - Australia

Edward Boutilier - Canada

Graham Merry - Canada

Andrzej Sawa - South Africa

Ian Ball - UK

Paul Evison - UK

John Philpott - UK

162

Ivan Cisar - Czech Republic

163

Chris Howes - UK

Bela Jansky - USA

164

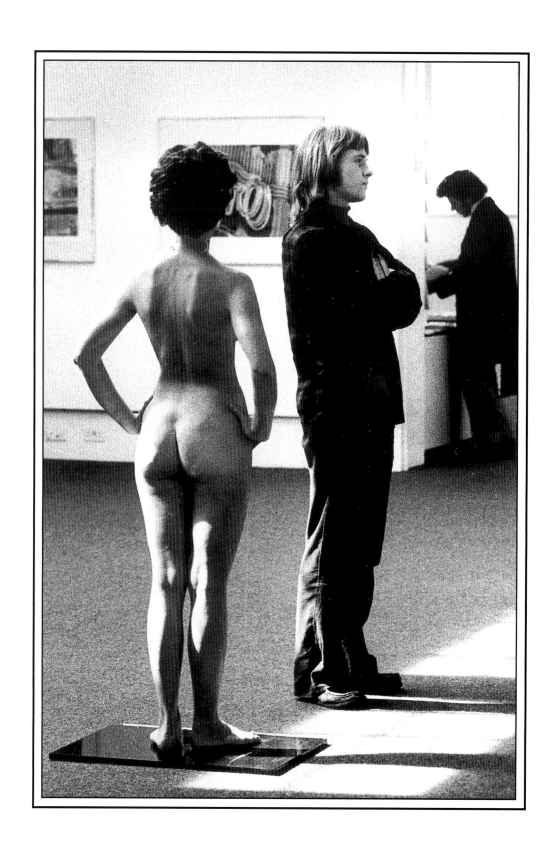

Robert Bailly - France

166

Rostvslav Kondrat - Ukraine

Hugh Milsom - UK

Hugh Milsom - UK

Alex Fyfe - UK

Clive Harrison - UK

Clive Harrison - UK

Dhiman Bose - India

174

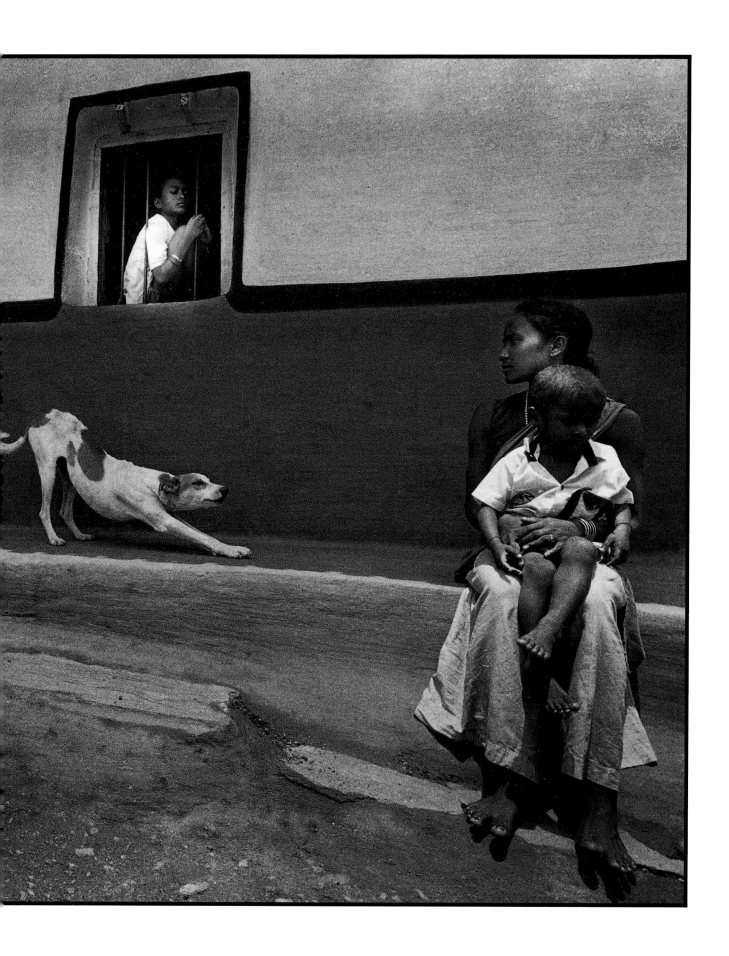

Krzsztof Grzelak - Poland

Eric Lancaster - UK

Fritz Pölking - Germany

Peter Gedeon - Hungary   *Augusto de Bernardi - Italy*

180

Bretislav Marek - Czech Republic

183

John Evans - UK

184

Norman Prue - UK

James Bidgood - UK

Tony Hamblin - UK

188

Tony Hamblin - UK

189

Paul Proctor - UK

190

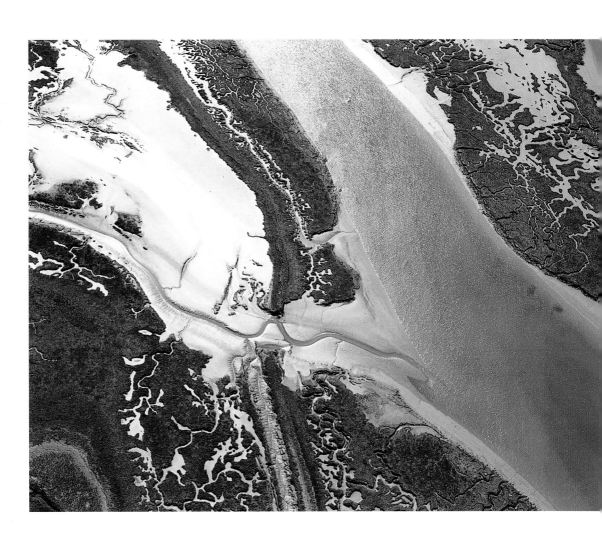

Paul Proctor - UK

191

Umberto Leonini - Italy

Gang Feng Wang - Canada

Guiseppe Pappalardo - Italy

John Bullough - UK

Carlo Chinca - UK

Peter Hense - Germany

198

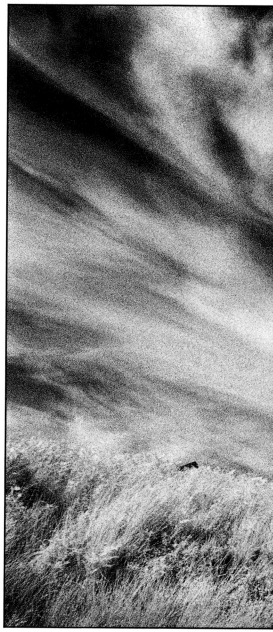

Arnold Hubbard - UK

200

Arnold Hubbard - UK

201

Aleksandras Macijauskas - Lithuania

202

Aleksandras Macijauskas - Lithuania

Brian Scott - Australia

Brian Scott - Australia

Alan Millward - UK

206

Alan Millward - UK

207

Andy Wilson - UK

Roger Noons - UK

209

Barrie Wilkins - South Africa

210

Barrie Wilkins - South Africa

211

Hezy Holzman - Israel

212

Hezy Holzman - Israel

Ulrich Ackermann - Switzerland

214

Ulrich Ackermann - Switzerland

215

Lip Seng Tan - Singapore

216

Donald Clements - UK

Laurie Campbell - UK

218

Laurie Campbell - UK

Nigel Amies - UK

John Gray - UK

Claudia Goetzelmann - Germany

222

Harry Hall - UK

224

TECHNICAL DATA

	COVER		**26**
Photographer	**Roger Noons (UK)**	Photographer	**Jill Sneesby (South Africa)**
	FRONT END PAPER		**27**
Photographer	**Leigh Preston (UK)**	Photographer	**Barrie Wilkins (South Africa)**
Subject/Location	**Aberystwyth, Wales**		
Camera	**Canon F1**		**28**
Lens	**Canon 70-200 mm zoom**	Photographer	**Roger Reynolds (UK)**
Film	**Ilford HP5**	Subject/Location	**Railway Worker, India**
	17		**29**
Photographer	**Barbro Bunnage (UK)**	Photographer	**Norman Prue (UK)**
Subject/Location	**Västerbotten, Sweden**	Subject/Location	**Audaipur Yard, Rajasthan**
Camera	**Nikon F801**	Camera	**Nikon F4**
Lens	**Nikkor 28-85 mm zoom**	Lens	**80-200 mm**
Film	**Fuji Velvia**	Film	**Kodachrome 64**
	18		**30**
Photographer	**Malcolm Beaumont (UK)**	Photographer	**David Cooke (UK)**
Subject/Location	**Woodland Crafts, West Sussex, England**	Camera	**Nikon FM2**
		Lens	**8 mm wide angle**
Camera	**Nikon FE**	Film	**Fuji 400D**
Lens	**20 mm**		
Film	**Kodachrome 64**		**31**
		Photographer	**Peter Jeffery (UK)**
	l9	Subject/Location	**Meadowhall Shopping Centre Precinct, Sheffield, England**
Photographer	**Malcolm Beaumont (UK)**		
Subject/Location	**Woodland Crafts, West Sussex, England**	Camera	**Canon T90**
		Lens	**7.5 mm wide angle**
Camera	**Nikon FE**	Film	**Ektachrome EPP**
Lens	**28 mm**		
Film	**Kodachrome 64**		**32**
		Photographer	**Ian George (UK)**
	20	Subject/Location	**Still Life**
Photographer	**Phil Dolby (UK)**	Camera	**Mamiya 645 Super**
Subject/Location	**Lanzou, China**	Lens	**80 mm**
Camera	**Canon EOS 600**	Film	**Fujichrome Real**
Lens	**28-70 mm**		
Film	**Fuji Velvia**		**33**
		Photographer	**Rod Edwards (UK)**
	21	Subject/Location	**Still Life on Slate**
Photographer	**Anthony Wharton (UK)**	Camera	**Mamiya 645 Super**
Subject/Location	**Switzerland**	Lens	**55 mm**
		Film	**Agfa 25**
	22		
Photographer	**Roger Cracknell (UK)**		**34**
Subject/Location	**Richmond Park, Surrey, England**	Photographer	**Chris Gleave (UK)**
Camera	**Hasselblad**	Subject/Location	**Manchester United v West Ham United**
Lens	**150 mm**		
Film	**Fuji Velvia**	Camera	**Canon EOS 1**
		Lens	**400 mm**
	23	Film	**Fuji Neopan 1600 (rated 3200)**
Photographer	**Nigel Shuttleworth (UK)**		
			35
	24	Photographer	**Chris Gleave (UK)**
Photographer	**Carolyn Bates (UK)**	Subject/Location	**Manchester United v Sheffield United**
Subject/Location	**Mud Woman, Asaro, Papua New Guinea**		
		Camera	**Canon EOS 1**
Camera	**Nikon F4**	Lens	**400 mm**
Lens	**80-200 mm**	Film	**Fuji Neopan 400**
Film	**Fujichrome 100**		
			36-37
	25	Photographer	**Clive Harrison (UK)**
Photographer	**Carolyn Bates (UK)**	Subject/Location	**Covent Garden, London**
Subject/Location	**Huli Warrior, Tari Basin, Papua New Guinea**	Camera	**Olympus OM1N**
		Lens	**100 mm**
Camera	**Nikon F4**	Film	**Ilford XP1**
Lens	**80-200 mm**		
Film	**Fujichrome 100**		

38

Photographer	Roy Elwood (UK)
Subject/Location	Routing Lenn, Northumberland
Camera	Bronica ETRS
Lens	75 mm
Film	Agfapan 25

39

Photographer	Roy Elwood (UK)
Subject/Location	Clashnessie, Scotland
Camera	Bronica ETRS
Lens	75 mm
Film	Ilford FP4

40

Photographer	Anne Crabbe (UK)
Camera	Olympus 35KC
Film	Kodak T-Max

41

Photographer	Tim Rudman (UK)

42

Photographer	Gang Feng Wang (Canada)
Camera	Nikon F3
Lens	50 mm

43

Photographer	Gang Feng Wang (Canada)
Camera	Easter
Film	Chinese

44-45

Photographer	Viktor Kolpakov (Latvia)

46

Photographer	Chris Howes (UK)
Subject/Location	Ogof Flynnon Cave, South Wales
Camera	Olympus OM1
Lens	35 mm
Film	Ilford FP4 with flash

47

Photographer	Chris Howes (UK)
Subject/Location	Arete Chamber in Ogof Flynnon Cave, South Wales
Camera	Olympus OMl
Lens	35 mm
Film	Ilford FP4 with flash

48

Photographer	Victor Attfield (UK)
Subject/Location	Sorrento, Italy
Camera	Nikkormat FT3
Lens	28 mm
Film	Kodak Tri-x

49

Photographer	Andrzej Sawa (South Africa)
Camera	Nikon F4
Lens	14 mm
Film	Fuji 100

50-51

Photographer	Kenneth Reay (UK)
Subject/Location	Ullswater, England
Camera	Bronica ETRS
Lens	75 mm
Film	Fuji Velvia

52-53

Photographer	Andreas Orfanos (Canada)
Subject/Location	Fasnacht, Basel, Switzerland
Camera	Nikon F4
Lens	35-70 mm zoom

54-55

Photographer	Den Reader (UK)
Subject/Location	Norfolk, England
Film	Kodachrome 64

56

Photographer	Dhiman Bose (India)

57

Photographer	Dhiman Bose (India)

58

Photographer	Frank Young (UK)

59

Photographer	Frank Young (UK)

60/61

Photographer	Norman Prue (UK)
Subject/Location	Thar Desert, Rajasthan
Camera	Nikon F4
Lens	80 mm
Film	Fuji Velvia

62

Photographer	Paul Mount (UK)
Camera	Nikon F4s
Lens	300 mm
Film	Fuji Velvia

63

Photographer	Mike Keegan (UK)
Camera	Canon EOS
Lens	100-300 mm zoom
Film	Fujichrome 100D

64

Photographer	Eugeni Komarov (Ukraine)

65

Photographer	Ivan Cisar (Czech Republic)

66

Photographer	Hugh Milsom (UK)
Subject/Location	Trees & Dyke, Snape, England
Camera	Canon AE
Lens	Tokina 24 mm
Film	Kodak Infra-red with Orange Filter

67

Photographer	Ray Spence (UK)
Subject/Location	Reeds, Cwm Bwchan, Wales
Camera	Mamiya RB 67
Lens	250 mm
Film	Ilford FP4

68

Photographer	Brian Tuff (UK)
Subject/Location	Bristol, England
Camera	Bronica ECTL
Lens	80 mm
Film	Ilford FP4

	69
Photographer	**Brian Tuff (UK)**
Subject/Location	**Bristol, England**
Camera	**Pentax 6x7**
Lens	**105 mm**
Film	**Ilford HP5**

	70/71
Photographer	**Leonid Padrul (Ukraine)**

	72-73
Photographer	**Ferenc Wagner (Hungary)**

	74
Photographer	**Carlo Chinca (UK)**
Subject/Location	**Holy Week, Malaga, Spain**
Camera	**Nikon F3**
Lens	**85 mm**
Film	**Ilford HP5**

	75
Photographer	**Carlo Chinca (UK)**
Subject/Location	**Holy Week, Spain**
Camera	**Nikon F3**
Lens	**20 mm**
Film	**Ilford HP5**

	76
Photographer	**Tim Rudman (UK)**

	77
Photographer	**Tim Rudman (UK)**

	78
Photographer	**Kazimieras Linkevicius (Lithuania)**
Camera	**Pentacon Six**
Lens	**120 mm**
Film	**Kodak FXP**

	79
Photographer	**Sergei Vosiliev (Russia)**
Subject/Location	**Moscow**
Camera	**Nikon F801**
Lens	**70-210 mm zoom**
Film	**A-2 400**

	80
Photographer	**Richard Searle (UK)**
Subject/Location	**Brinkworth, Wiltshire, England**
Camera	**Canon AE1**
Lens	**50 mm**
Film	**Ilford FP4**

	81
Photographer	**Malcolm Pleasants (UK)**
Subject/Location	**Amsterdam, Netherlands**
Camera	**Minolta Dynax 7000**
Lens	**28 mm**
Film	**Fuji 1600**

	82-83
Photographer	**Rosemary Calvert (UK)**
Subject/Location	**Grizzley Bears, USA**
Camera	**Canon EOS 10s**
Lens	**28-80 mm zoom**
Film	**Fuji Velvia 50**

	84-85
Photographer	**Mike Taylor (UK)**
Subject/Location	**Carnival, Paranagua, Brazil**
Camera	**Olympus XA**
Film	**Agfachrome R1000S**

	86
Photographer	**Johann Froschauer (Austria)**

	87
Photographer	**Robert Kudlik (Switzerland)**

	88
Photographer	**E A Janes (UK)**
Subject/Location	**Wildebeest at dawn, Amboseli, Kenya**

	89
Photographer	**Fritz Pölking (Germany)**
Subject/Location	**Cheetahs in Masai Mara, Kenya**
Camera	**Nikon F4**
Lens	**400 mm**
Film	**Fuji 400**

	90-91
Photographer	**Athanas Gritzer (Austria)**

	92
Photographer	**Peter Siviter (UK)**
Subject/Location	**Bognor Regis, England**

	93
Photographer	**Mike Keegan (UK)**
Camera	**Canon**
Lens	**100-200 mm zoom**
Film	**Fujichrome 100D**

	94-95
Photographer	**Peter Roche (UK)**
Subject/Location	**Mauritius**
Camera	**Nikon F3**
Lens	**20 mm**
Film	**Ektachrome 100 Plus**

	96
Photographer	**Roger Noons (UK)**

	97
Photographer	**Romualdas Rakauskas (Lithuania)**
Camera	**Nikon E3**
Lens	**35 mm**
Film	**A25**

	98-99
Photographer	**Brian Tuff (UK)**
Subject/Location	**Avebury, Wiltshire, England**
Camera	**Canon A1**
Lens	**24 mm**
Film	**Kodak Infra-red**

	100-101
Photographer	**Gang Feng Wang (Canada)**
Camera	**Nikon F3**
Lens	**50 mm**

	102/103
Photographer	Andy Hoets (USA)
Subject/Location	Central Park, New York City
Camera	Leica M4
Lens	35 mm
Film	Kodak Infra-red

	104
Photographer	Max Johnson (Australia)
Subject/Location	Sydney, Australia
Camera	Nikon F4
Lens	105 mm
Film	Kodak T-Max 400

	105
Photographer	Max Johnson (Australia)
Subject/Location	Sydney, Australia
Camera	Nikon F4
Lens	70-210 mm zoom
Film	Kodak T-Max 400

	106-107
Photographer	Pavlo Drobjak (Ukraine)

	108
Photographer	Roger Hance (UK)
Subject/Location	Birmingham, England
Camera	Canon T90
Lens	24 mm
Film	Kodak Delta 400 rated at 1600

	109
Photographer	Fabio Ponzio (Italy)
Subject/Location	Warsaw, Poland
Camera	Nikon F4
Lens	28 mm
Film	Kodak T-Max

	110-111
Photographer	Chris Hinterobermaier (Austria)

	112-113
Photographer	Manfred Hermann (Germany)

	114-115
Photographer	Ulrich Ackermann (Switzerland)

	116
Photographer	Clare Glenister (UK)

	117
Photographer	George Ghiz (Canada)

	118-119
Photographer	Carli Dietmar (Austria)

	120
Photographer	Manfred Pillik (Austria)

	121
Photographer	Jan Svendsen (Norway)
Subject/Location	Late Evening
Camera	Nikon F601
Film	Fujichrome

	122-123
Photographer	Augusto De Bernardi (Italy)

	124-125
Photographer	Sue Bennett

	126
Photographer	Robert Kralka (Canada)
Subject/Location	Toronto, Canada
Camera	Nikon FE2
Lens	300 mm
Film	Ektachrome 100

	127
Photographer	Robert Kralka (Canada)
Subject/Location	Toronto, Canada
Camera	Nikon FE2
Lens	200 mm
Film	Fujichrome 100

	128
Photographer	Athanas Gritzer (Austria)

	129
Photographer	Alex Fyfe (UK)
Subject/Location	George Melly
Camera	Pentax ME Super
Lens	70-210 mm zoom
Film	Ilford HP5

	130-131
Photographer	Brian Scott (Australia)
Subject/Location	Summer Horse Trials, Durmore, Australia
Camera	Nikon FM2
Lens	300 mm
Film	Kodak T-Max 400

	132-133
Photographer	John Anthony (UK)
Subject/Location	Zaire
Camera	Leica MP4
Lens	35 mm
Film	Ilford HP5

	134/135
Photographer	Boris Panov (Ukraine)

	136-137
Photographer	Pavel Kunin (Kazakhstan)
Camera	Zenit Gelios - 44

	138/139
Photographer	Joe Tymkow (UK)
Subject/Location	London
Camera	Fujica ST 60SN
Lens	135 mm
Film	Ilford HP5

	140
Photographer	Markus Lauboeck (Austria)
Camera	Minolta 7000i
Lens	35-70 mm zoom
Film	Ilford XP2

	141
Photographer	Reinhold Rothschedl (Austria)

142-143	
Photographer	Leigh Preston (UK)
Subject/Location	Sutherland, England
Camera	Canon F1
Lens	24 mm
Film	Ilford HP5

144	
Photographer	Mike Hollist (UK)
Subject/Location	Port Lympne Zoo, England
Camera	Nikon F2
Lens	180 mm
Film	Kodak Tri-x

145	
Photographer	Mike Hollist (UK)
Subject/Location	Guildford, England
Camera	Nikon F2
Lens	85 mm
Film	Kodak 160

146	
Photographer	Roger Reynolds (UK)

147	
Photographer	Roger Reynolds (UK)

148	
Photographer	Damian Debski (UK)
Subject/Location	Young Anubis Baboon

149	
Photographer	Julie Meech (UK)
Subject/Location	Mother and Baby Baboon, Kenya
Camera	Pentax K1000
Lens	100 mm
Film	Kodachrome 64

150-151	
Photographer	Lisa Benstead (UK)
Subject/Location	Zaire
Camera	Minolta Dynax 3xi
Lens	70-210 mm zoom
Film	Kodak 400

152	
Photographer	Bill Ivy (Canada)
Subject/Location	Common Loon with Fish, Ontario, Canada
Camera	Canon RT
Lens	100-300 mm zoom
Film	Kodachrome 64

153	
Photographer	Bill Ivy (Canada)
Subject/Location	Common Loon, Haliburton, Ontario, Canada
Camera	Canon F1
Lens	85-300 mm zoom
Film	Kodachrome 64

154	
Photographer	Anthony Wharton (UK)
Subject/Location	Clent Hills, Worcester, England

155	
Photographer	Van Greaves (UK)
Subject/Location	Kenver Edge, Staffs, England
Camera	Nikon F801
Lens	24 mm plus polariser
Film	Fujichrome

156	
Photographer	Bob Mossel (Australia)

157	
Photographer	Edward Boutilier (Canada)

158	
Photographer	Graham Merry (Canada)
Subject/Location	Vancouver, Canada
Camera	Nikonos V
Lens	28 mm

159	
Photographer	Andrzej Sawa (South Africa)
Camera	Nikon F4
Lens	24 mm
Film	Fuji 100

160	
Photographer	Ian Ball (UK)
Subject/Location	Schaun Baker - Free Fall World Record Holder Canoeist, 45 feet fall - Wales
Camera	Nikon F4s
Lens	85 mm

161	
Photographer	Paul Evison (UK)
Subject/Location	Nottingham
Camera	Nikon FE
Lens	180 mm
Film	Kodak Tri-x

162	
Photographer	John Philpott (UK)
Camera	Olympus OM2N
Lens	28 mm
Film	Kodak T-Max 400

163	
Photographer	Ivan Cisar (Czech Republic)

164	
Photographer	Chris Howes (UK)
Subject/Location	Cross Country Skiing, Brecon Beacons
Camera	Olympus OM4
Lens	24 mm
Film	Ilford FP4

165	
Photographer	Bela Jansky (USA)
Subject/Location	Gulmarg, Kashmir, India
Camera	Canon FTB
Lens	28 mm
Film	Eastman Color

	166
Photographer	Robert Bailly (France)
Subject/Location	Hyperrealist Exhibition, Serpentine Gallery, London
Camera	Leica M5
Lens	35 mm
Film	Ilford HP4

	167
Photographer	Rostvslav Kondrat (Ukraine)

	168
Photographer	Hugh Milsom (UK)
Subject/Location	Great Amwell, Hertfordshire, England
Camera	Canon AE
Lens	24 mm with orange filter
Film	Kodak Infra-red

	169
Photographer	Hugh Milsom (UK)
Subject/Location	Derbyshire, England
Camera	Canon AE
Lens	24 mm
Film	Kodak Infra-red

	170/171
Photographer	Alex Fyfe (UK)
Camera	Pentax ME Super
Lens	70-210 mm zoom
Film	Ilford HP5

	172
Photographer	Clive Harrison (UK)
Subject/Location	Blackheath, England
Camera	Olympus OM1N
Lens	50 mm
Film	Ilford XP1

	173
Photographer	Clive Harrison (UK)
Subject/Location	Dog Show, Richmond, Surrey, England
Camera	Olympus OM1N
Lens	100 mm
Film	Ilford XP1

	174/175
Photographer	Dhiman Bose (India)

	176
Photographer	Krzsztof Grzelak (Poland)
Camera	Nikon FE2
Lens	85 mm
Film	Fotopan HL

	177
Photographer	Eric Lancaster (UK)
Subject/Location	Moscow
Camera	Minolta Dynax 7000i
Lens	70-210 mm zoom
Film	Fuji

	178-179
Photographer	Fritz Pölking (Germany)
Subject/Location	Cheetahs, Masai Mara, Kenya
Camera	Nikon F4
Lens	300 mm
Film	Fuji Velvia 50

	180
Photographer	Peter Gedeon (Hungary)
Subject/Location	National Park, Bükk, Hungary
Camera	Minolta XD-7
Lens	16 mm
Film	Fuji RVP

	181
Photographer	Augusto de Bernardi (Italy)

	182-183
Photographer	Bretislav Marek (Czech Republic)

	184
Photographer	John Evans (UK)
Subject/Location	Goree Island, Dakar

	185
Photographer	Norman Prue (UK)
Subject/Location	Washday at Udaipur Railway Yard, Rajasthan
Camera	Nikon F4
Lens	80-200 mm zoom
Film	Kodachrome 64

	186/187
Photographer	James Bidgood (UK)

	188
Photographer	Tony Hamblin (UK)
Subject/Location	Great Blue Heron

	189
Photographer	Tony Hamblin (UK)
Subject/Location	Great White Heron

	190
Photographer	Paul Proctor (UK)
Subject/Location	Piccadilly Circus, London
Camera	Pentax 6x7
Lens	105 mm
Film	Ektacolor Gold

	191
Photographer	Paul Proctor (UK)
Subject/Location	The Blackwater Estuary, Essex, England
Camera	Pentax 6x7
Lens	105 mm
Film	Ektacolor Gold

	192
Photographer	Umberto Leonini (Italy)

	193
Photographer	Gang Feng Wang (Canada)
Camera	Nikon F3
Lens	80-200 mm zoom

	194/195
Photographer	Giuseppe Pappalardo (Italy)
Subject/Location	Paris
Camera	Leica M6
Film	Agfa APX 100

196
Photographer · John Bullough (UK)
Subject/Location · Explosion at MEP Station,
Hereford, England
Camera · Nikon FE2
Film · Ilford FP4

197
Photographer · Carlo Chinca (UK)
Camera · Nikon F3
Lens · 135 mm
Film · Ilford HP5

198
Photographer · Peter Hense (Germany)
Subject/Location · Apollo Theatre, Harlem, New York
Camera · Nikon 801s
Lens · 135 mm
Film · Kodak T-Max 100

199
Photographer · Peter Hense (Germany)
Subject/Location · New York
Camera · Nikon 801s
Lens · 85 mm
Film · Kodak T-Max 100

200
Photographer · Arnold Hubbard (UK)
Subject/Location · Scargill Church, Kettlewell,
Yorkshire Dales
Camera · Nikon FE
Lens · 20 mm
Film · Kodak Infra-red

201
Photographer · Arnold Hubbard (UK)
Subject/Location · Embleton, Northumbria, England
Camera · Nikon FE
Lens · 20 mm
Film · Kodak Infra-red

202-203
Photographer · Aleksandras Macijauskas (Lithuania)
Camera · Nikon F
Lens · 28 mm
Film · Foto 130

204-205
Photographer · Brian Scott (Australia)
Camera · Nikon FM2
Lens · 500 mm
Film · Kodak T-Max 400

206
Photographer · Alan Millward (UK)
Subject/Location · Bikaner Railway Station, Rajasthan
Camera · Canon T90
Lens · 50 mm
Film · Kodak Tri-X

207
Photographer · Alan Millward (UK)
Subject/Location · Udaipur, Rajasthan
Camera · Canon T90
Lens · 20 mm
Film · Kodak Tri-X

208
Photographer · Andy Wilson (UK)
Camera · Nikon F301
Lens · 24 mm
Film · Ilford XP2

209
Photographer · Roger Noons (UK)

210-211
Photographer · Barrie Wilkins (South Africa)

212-213
Photographer · Hezy Holzman (Israel)

214-215
Photographer · Ulrich Ackermann (Switzerland)

216
Photographer · Lip Seng Tan (Singapore)

217
Photographer · Donald Clements (UK)

218
Photographer · Laurie Campbell (UK)
Subject/Location · Oak Seedling

219
Photographer · Laurie Campbell (UK)

220-221
Photographer · Nigel Amies (UK)

222
Photographer · John Gray (UK)

223
Photographer · Claudia Goetzelmann (Germany)
Subject/Location · South Togo
Camera · Nikon F4
Lens · 35-70 mm zoom

224
Photographer · Harry Hall (UK)

BACK END PAPER
Photographer · Steve Woodgate (UK)
Camera · Olympus OM40
Lens · Tokina 70-210 mm zoom
Film · Ilford HP5

Steve Woodgate - UK